RIOT IN THE CHARM FACTORY

Todd Colby

RIOT IN THE CHARM FACTORY

New and Selected Work

TODD COLBY

Includes Selections from *Cush* and *Ripsnort*

Introduction by Bob Holman

ACKNOWLEDGMENTS

Think Eight and *The Incidents* were first published by *Fatstick Magazine,* edited by James Wilk. *Gotham Selectric Miniatures* was written on an I.B.M. Selectric while working at Gotham Bookmart spring of 1997.

Portions of this book previously appeared as hand-made xerographic editions *Ripsnort* and *Cush,* published by Soft Skull Press, at the 12th Street Kinko's, in 1994 & 1995.

Some of the material in *Cush* first appeared in various magazines and on CD, including publications: *Cocodrilo, Caspar Weinberger: The Hot Pants Anthology, Monster Trucks*; and CDs: *Poemfone Volume One: New Word Order* and *Live at Eureka Joe: Family Matters.*

Some of the material in *Ripsnort* first appeared in magazines *Longshot, Waterfront Weekly,* and *Interview.*

Cover Photograph: Jem Cohen.
Author Photograph: David Taffet.
Editorial: Cynthia Nelson, Sander Hicks.

THANKS

Jem Cohen, David Taffet, Bob Holman, Maggie Estep, Elizabeth Zechel, Lisa Colby, Dana Albarella, Justin Theroux, Marianne Vitale, Michael Portnoy, David Lantow, Seth Markel, Gabriel Cohen, Michael Colby, Cynthia Nelson, Sander Hicks, Bookcourt, and The Poetry Project at St. Mark's Church.

SUPPORT

Questions, comments or problems with your new book of poems?
Contact *Riot in the Charm Factory* Tech Support:
charmfactory1@aol.com

WWW.SOFTSKULL.COM

to d. boon

TABLE OF CONTENTS

Introduction by Bob Holman iii

I. *Charm Factory*

Eat Me 1
Thanks a Bunch 3
Ass Life 5
Stiff Prick 7
Captain's Log 9
The Boy And The Girl 11
Ken And Kathy 19
Notes Home 23
Angels 25
Jackass 27
Gotham Selectric Miniatures 29
Gods Fight With Pink Fists 31
Peach Pit/Bully Pulpit 33
Miracle Conference .35
The Incidents 37
The Speed of Light: A Message 41
Towers of My Appreciation 43
The Candy 45
Dear, I Love 49
Alien Lemon Egg 51
If God Lives Inside of Us 57
Void Where Prohibited By Law 59
Think Eight 61
She Was Red 63
The Industry Standard 65
I Was Able or My Life as I Recall It 67

II. *Cush*

My Music 75
Tug 77
Imperial Crown 79
Hotel Valium 81
Surprise 83
Pineapple, Sandalwood, & Marzipan 85
Boys Town 87

Hollow 89
Twenty Songs for My Unborn Fifth Child 91
Buy 93
Insomnia 95
Pink Syncopation 97
Cinamon 99
Unbronzed Fret 101

III. *Ripsnort*

Bull by the Horns 107
Cowboy Poem 109
What's for Dreamer 111
Bronze Poem 113
Come 115
Another Kiss Poem 117
Cake 119
The Boss 121
Blue Poem 125

INTRODUCTION

*"The power of prominence has a special
bloated charm that tends to exacerbate as
well as dishevel a person, heck, some
might even say it destroys the soul..."*
—Todd Colby

It's always the same. Somebody, just back from a poetry reading, calls me in a panic: seems there was this poet there who looked like just this regular guy, standing shyly at the mic and then he opened his mouth and then OUT COMES THIS SPEW OF NASTY LAVA BARKING AND BRAYING...OBSCENE AND HILARIOUS AND UNQUENCHABLE and it turns out the guy was not a poet at all. He was a serial killer!

Welcome to Todd Colby's pain.

On MTV they cast him as the boiler repair guy whose features Francis Baconize before your eyes. Lead throat for band Drunken Boat found him sniffing all armpits while bellowing in unknown languages. On "Words in Your Face" for PBS he advocated using a cat as a dairy animal ("Hold them above your cereal and SQUEEZE.") As Hindi Narrator for the Yogurt Boys (with Michael Portnoy and Marianne Vitale) he engages in weird sex while encased in a tin foil Michelin suit (the Yogurt Boys' epic, "The Boy and the Girl," is one of the highlights of these pages). At St. Mark's Poetry Project they handed over the Wednesday Night Reading series to him and watched as he appeared as the madder professor, churning up the best minds in the country. His rants gave Jordan Trachtenberg the idea for PoemFone, and Jordy returned the favor by decreeing the first three days of every month Todd's property, "The Todd Colby Buffer Zone."

The world is "The Todd Colby Buffer Zone" and we're not really doing all that well, buffering, I mean. The anger that drives the world is Todd Colby's poetry. It thrives sweet like candy and tinkles like a charm bracelet, while its image is a close-up of bared fangs on a balloon neck. When it goes pop all the evil shit runs out. That's when I get the phone call: "LAVA! LAVA!"

I tell 'em, settle down, I will send something to soothe thy Poor, Burned Soule. And what I send 'em is a copy of one of Todd Colby's books.

Because the secret is that the poems upon which Todd builds these mighty volcanoes of roar are in actuality tightly constructed codices of delight. In order to explode, Todd first creates the things themselves. That's where the books come in.

Riot in the Charm Factory moves from poem to fiction to reportage, from the grinning skull of Poe to Lenny Bruce's adenoids to a rhythm of repetition that is entirely Colby and goes like this: Say it, since nobody's listening ("Are you even listening?" from "Think Eight"), say it again a little different ("Would it be better if that's what it was all about: listening?"), since your anger is now louder than the silence of the nonlistening you break it down and repeat and re-form till it's like this dance that can't stop, this cementmixer you cannot escape from, the eternal pound. Hallelujah! I'm a (Todd Colby) poem!

It's why he can say, in "Great Word: Audit." In fact, "Audit" is the whole poem. Because—it is said, "Aw, dit!" And because "Audit" starts auditory, which is a great way to get "Audit" across. And because, as poet, Todd knows what else is great about "Audit," which is, if an actual audit should befall, it's someone else they befall upon. What a GREAT WORD, to happen to somebody else.

But everything else, alas, falls on Todd Colby, our Job. Todd Colby, this is your ass life. For our sins, what he does is fall asleep on the floor in front of the television with his hand in an empty Doritos bag: 2:54 a.m.

The tension of the murderous performer vs. the tightly packed poetic form lets Todd do his famous Rooster Walk: God. It's a spiritual thing. Totally uncool to invoke God post-mod. But in the blender that is Todd's whirling art spasm, God herself is continually spinning out, actually being created, visioned, visited. There's a way in which Todd's poems, blasphemous and heinous and pus-filled and covered with mugwort and lysergic acid as they are, are all prayers.

And he's praying for all of us.

BOB HOLMAN
NYC, 1999

"It could end at anytime and you just try not to be afraid."
—*Rudy Burkhardt*

"It may be pointless to speak in a general way about the living conditions of poets."
—*Bataille*

EAT ME

I believe that all dreamers enter the picture on their knees.
If they are wise it is hard going and toxic
but hardly a reason to engulf one's self in flames—
After all, gasoline is flammable and can do great harm.

But the possibilities of harm are minimized
here in the all new effervescent zone
where the capacity for love is eternal
if you believe in rising up to the stars
with gum shoes and peachy keen liquor breath.

With a genuine motor-mouth you can cut through
all this while staying hell bent for leather.
These are milestones, and there's a commotion
on the horizon that you can smell long before you see.

Any planet will do, just pick one that is preferably
built on a solid wooden platform so that you can
dance on it like the little shit you are.

You are close enough to smell the air
where a triple spin is worth a thousand points.
In the middle of dinner you are nothing—
You know nothing, so there.
After all, thunder is amusing and lightening is pretty wild
until it strikes you and then you just have to die.

If the oxygen you need is greater than your ability
to breathe, then you have reached an actual aerobic limit—
So perhaps at that point you should back off
before more damage is done to your brain.

Here's the point:

If you look dashing with a wish smeared across your face
perhaps you'll be confused with the dreamer
as you lap at the bitter water. Zone in on me.
Clean me. I want you to lick me. This might be the weight.
This might be the night. This might be a little of both
where the props have actually flipped in the dark.

THANKS A BUNCH

I was surprised that you claimed I only work for you. On the contrary, I'm the person who is pressing charges against you. When you indicated that you did not know who wrote the threatening letter, and you did not press charges, I flipped the switch on the rod and let the line go as far as I wanted.

It was not me yelping and breaking bottles outside your house though you seemed to indicate to the authorities that it was me, that was a mistake on your behalf and I hope you can live with it just as I have had to live with it. It seems to me that we could iron things out without my having to bite you, though I am still the one pressing charges on you. I can live with the mistake, but only if you understand I was surprised you claimed I only work for you. The people working on this problem for me see what a mistake you made when you indicated that you did not know. You know, and you know you know.

I want you to know right now that if you ever touch my cheek again I'll bite your hand down to the bone—where my teeth will be crushing the bones in your hand. I hope you won't let the contents of this letter get in between us. Just imagine if you never heard from me again, how would you live with that? I was hoping we could get together over one of the many holidays spread throughout the year and talk about the old days.

ASS LIFE

Oh here's something really great: my ass life.
And when I get tired of it I can always
"blah blah blah." And the cigarettes we use
when fighting our little wars are marble
so we don't actually have to smoke them
we just suck on them and they look pretty
amazing until the enemy arrives
and then it's just more "blah blah blah."
A hand in a sock entitled "The Puppet."
I pour gravy on the bed
and none of you seem too thrilled
about being enthralled by such a mess
but I think it's an artistic revenge scheme
carried to the limit of recognizable light.
We stick our hands in our pockets,
suck our cigarettes, and smile
as much as we can.
It's raining all the time now
so it's good we can muster up the will
to be outside and to succumb
to the throbbing will.
If I were invisible
then I wouldn't have to do math.
The token didn't work for me
because it was invisible.
It was not a treat to explain my "Invisible Theory"
to the police officers.
Sunny sand and stars.
This is my ass life,
fuck it.

STIFF PRICK

1.

There is a stink that comes out of him. He smells like a farmer who has worked in a fog of his own jack-off death juices when he comes into the house to chow down on some grub.

Some days there's not much to look at in the house so when they dim the lights his prick gets stiff.

A woman pushes a rusty steel cart down the center aisle of the house. She collects tiny scabs and dried skin as she strokes his back. She puts the pieces of his body that are cast off in an old wooden bucket. His prick gets stiff when she grooms him.

With his face in an old mashed pillow, he counts the things he sees thousands of feet below on the surface of the earth. All he can see are lights where the roads are. Her voice is in his head. He can't remember what she looks like anymore. His prick gets stiff as he imagines her riding his bike over a wooden ramp and jumping over some old garbage cans.

In the summer it is easier to smell when the farmer is home.

While he drank orange juice or chewed a piece of bacon he could stiffen his own prick.

A big wind could blow through the house at any moment and stiffen his best looking prick. As always, he has the pleasure of floating when his prick is stiff. It's possible he's floating in a place no one else would be able to understand. She is beside herself whenever she sees him stiffen his own prick by grinding his hips into the bed. They've hit turbulence. "Like a deep blue thunderstorm."

Blinding white light. Cardboard cut out and sewn together to make a brown pyramid on the seat of a chair. Someday someone humming a certain tune will bring you to tears. Your prick will be stiff as you listen, crying into the crook of your arm, ashamed.

He's trying to throw a paper airplane with his stiff prick. He's looking at all the products on the market that can modify the serotonin levels in his brain. Wind blows dirt and dried leaves past his stiff prick.

2.

He sticks his stiff prick in the car door and slams it in there while neighbors chat on the stoop next door. He pulls out his stiff prick, shoves it at them and says "hey look!" and they see his stiff prick and then he says "watch!" which means the same thing as "hey look!" He gets out of his car and slams his stiff prick in the door and then he opens the window in his house with his stiff prick and he says "hey look!" and he gets in the car and slams the door on his stiff prick and then he says "stiff prick" and he slams the door on it "hey look stiff prick" and he opens the door and his stiff prick is in the door he slams it "the sky blue prick" he slams it in the car door and burns a candle and drips hot wax on his stiff prick.

Wall to wall shining. The neighbors are shocked. A wide swath of stiff prick. He is furious now his "heart is pounding" stiff prick in the car door. If you see it say "hello stiff prick" and so he says "wait for my stiff prick, there's some really nice news I have for you," slamming his stiff prick in the car door.

CAPTAIN'S LOG

Thought of a dear friend: 1:54 AM

Side ache from leaning over in conversation with myself: 2:12 AM

Videotaped myself dancing with my shirt off: 2:17 AM

Realized I look like a jerk dancing with my shirt off: 2:25 AM

Purchased a cherry pie from the deli: 4:46 AM

Ate entire cherry pie in despair: 5.04 AM

Touched myself with improper things: 5:52 AM

Fell asleep in a cold sweat: 6:05 AM

Woke up and ate the last of the chocolate chip cookies: 1:35 PM

Walked to work: 1:45 PM

Pissed into a co-worker's coffee cup in the employee's bathroom: 2:10 PM

Made a crude noose from a belt: 6:43 PM

Cleared the patio for a beheading: 9:28 PM

Looked for a new job: 10:17 PM

Called someone and hung up: 12 midnight.

Sprawled face-down on the living room floor: 1:12 AM

Ate corn flakes with heavy cream: 2:07 AM

Fell asleep on the floor in front of the television with my hand in an empty Doritos bag: 2:54 AM

THE BOY AND THE GIRL

1. The boy and the girl loved each other very much. They saw the world in a very similar way so they didn't have to do too much extraneous translating or explaining to each other about what they saw or felt. They could take certain things for granted because they spoke the same language. They were not morons. They loved each other so much that they quit their jobs and hired people to do the things that they could no longer be bothered to do. They paid their bills on time and took great pleasure in watching the workers do the jobs that they had done under great duress, only months before. At the orientation meeting for the workers the boy and the girl instructed them to clap together on the count of three. They called this the "We're-All-One Clap" because they didn't want any of the workers to be alienated by the exclusivity of their love for each other.

2. There was a certain confidence that the boy and the girl had that came from choking each other while fucking, and this "confidence" was evident in the way they addressed the workers at the orientation meeting.

3. The boy and the girl started speaking a secret language which didn't address the larger issue of the unease they both felt whenever they spoke their language to the workers. There were too many obscure or syrupy phrases and many of their words had meanings that shifted around a lot. The workers reacted to all this by making marks in their ledgers every time a dog barked, which allowed them to maintain contact with the real world.

4. Question: How many individual dog barks does the average person hear in a lifetime?
Answer: 18,841 *woofs*.

5. Many nights the boy and the girl would sit in bed naked and plot out ways that they could eat each other without getting the wounds infected or running out of flesh to eat.

6. The borders between them started to blur, and in the aftermath of this "blurring" the boy and the girl became even more alienated from the workers. Because the workers couldn't understand the couple's language with its sugary baby talk, they stopped listening to their commands—so they had absolutely no idea what they were being told to do. Needless to say, it didn't take long before things started looking pretty shabby around the compound.

7. The boy and the girl started to look Rubenesque and smudged.

8. It was around this time that the workers' unwillingness to do their chores centered around a mysterious blue gas that entered the room through the air ducts whenever the boy and girl gave them orders.

9. The boy and the girl decided to see a Specialist to help them with their "special problems."

10. When they went to the Specialist, she told them that their problems were due to some repressed anguish or mutual self-destructive desire that would cost a lot of money to find out more about.

11. The boy and the girl started getting anxious when the workers began doing their morning "We're-All-One-Clap" with an absurd amount of enthusiasm.

12. On one occasion the girl referred to the boy as "criminally charismatic" in front of the workers. Later that evening a half-dozen or so of the workers got drunk around a fire and told scary stories that all ended with the naive couple getting hacked up with machetes. When they got tired of telling their stories with the same endings, they took turns imitating the girl saying "criminally charismatic" while another worker would pretend to be the boy with his sheepish, theatrically-embarrassed grin.

13. The boy and the girl interpreted the workers' growing hostility towards them as sexual which could only be alleviated by a really good fucking.

14. One morning while watching the workers perform their "We're-All-One Clap" the boy turned to the girl and asked "Who would you really like to fuck right now?" To which the girl replied "Why you, of course." The workers heard this exchange and made a mental note of it for later use.

15. The words that came out of the boy's mouth were the same as the ones that came out of the girl's mouth so they were able to express certain things to each other as long as they understood who was really doing the talking.

16. The girl turned to the boy and said "I think I'll have you for dinner tonight." While the boy was mildly turned-on by this idea, he was also afraid of actually being consumed by the girl against his will. But it was only a passing feeling.

17. The boy and the girl each believed they'd been sent for each other by some sort of divine command. When they confessed this to the Specialist she seemed to agree but warned them of possible mutual ruination if they confessed it to anyone else.

18. The girl started to smell of bleach, so the boy asked the girl about it and she told him not to worry because all geniuses smell like bleach. From that moment on the boy didn't let the smell bother him anymore for fear that she might not think him her equal.

19. The boy and the girl each knew that the first sign of immortality is becoming invisible to dogs. The second sign of immortality is the ability to hear funk instead of barks when a dog opens its mouth.

20. The Specialist reminded the boy and the girl to watch some of the television shows that the networks had taken the trouble to make for their enjoyment.

21. The girl turned to the boy as they left the Specialist's office and said, "We should watch some of the shows tonight." At which point the boy reminded the girl of something else the Specialist had said: "Nothing done out of anxiety will ever work."

22. The boy and the girl wanted to eat each other's genitals so they'd stick their heads in between each other's legs and grunt and slurp as though they were pigs eating musk-scented slop. While the couple made their noises behind their locked bedroom door, the workers would stand outside and snicker, knowing full well that they could break into the room and slaughter the couple if they really wanted to.

23. After fucking all day the boy fell asleep and had a dream that the girl had a honeycomb the size of a dinner roll attached to the back of her neck. Inside the chambers of the honeycomb were tiny mustard colored pellets that fell out whenever she spoke. He woke up from the dream and checked the back of her neck as she slept to make sure it wasn't for real.

24. On the same night the girl had a dream that she couldn't rest her head on the pillow because a dinner roll was attached to the back of her neck. The Specialist told them that this meant they were visiting each other in their dreams—which is one of the benefits of watching television together.

25. The next morning the boy got up early and begged one of the friendlier workers to make a T-shirt for the girl that said "THE BOY HAD A DREAM ABOUT ME AND ALL HE BROUGHT BACK WAS THIS LOUSY T-SHIRT."

26. The girl didn't seem to understand that if the boy started bringing actual objects back from his dreams he'd wind up having a nervous breakdown.

27. That morning the boy and the girl watched a rerun of the first lunar landing on television. As they sat curled up together on the sofa, the girl wore the T-shirt that the boy had begged a friendly worker to make for her.

28. One evening while the girl was bathing, the boy looked through her drawers hoping to find some evidence that she was misleading him about her real identity. While there were several books about television celebrities hidden away in an old shoe box, he didn't find anything that was too much out of the ordinary. As he put everything back in its proper place he felt a yucky feeling in his stomach which made him think he'd betrayed her. When the girl came back into the room she had no idea what the boy had been doing moments before, so she kissed him gently on the forehead, which put the boy at ease for the time being.

29. Several days later the girl explained to the boy how some lovers will slowly start to look alike and that eventually, no one would be able to tell them apart. Someday, she told him, the workers would-

n't even know which one of them was giving them their commands. She went on to explain what wonderful tricks they could play with their new identities. The boy thought that wasn't such a bad thing—but the idea of her going through his drawers and questioning his identity made him shiver a bit. At that very moment he noticed that her cheeks did sort of look like his, and their eyes were already the same color, so they were on their way towards some sort of total love transformation.

30. The boy started to imagine that the girl was secretly putting poison in his food and drink. He started to distract the girl before eating their meals so that he could switch the plates and glasses before she noticed. This way, he thought, he would never be poisoned.

31. Once, when they were sitting in the gazebo by the pool, the girl brought him a margarita which he absentmindedly drank without switching drinks with her. Nothing happened, so he felt a sudden rush of love for the girl.

32. The specialist told the couple that when they were walking around the city they should constantly ask themselves who they would really like to fuck at that very moment.

33. Two of the workers were spying on the boy and the girl when they saw them fucking next to the pool on a lawn chair that collapsed just as they were climaxing. That night the two workers reenacted the exact same scene for the other workers who became sexually aroused as they watched.

34. When the boy and the girl sat down at the end of the day to watch the television, color leaked out onto the linoleum floor of their family room. Fast cars on the screen made hot pink sounds, while love scenes spilled out a cool blue color. The boy and the girl initially found this rather amusing, but the workers, who had to

clean up the mess around the television, grew very irritated with the situation.

35. The workers sent a fax to the boy and the girl that said "We like your lips as long as they kiss when they speak." The boy and the girl were confused by the message and asked themselves how they could possibly say anything if they were always kissing.

36. The boy and the girl decided to withdraw deeper into their own language so they stopped going outside at all. After a few days of not seeing the boy and the girl strolling around the compound, the workers barricaded the couple inside their room and left the premises to look for other work.

37. Inside their room, the boy and the girl glued seashells to the walls in elaborate patterns. There was no water, so they cut a tiny hole in the window that they would gently lick when it rained. When it got cold they burned their clothes not so much for the warmth as for the brilliant multicolored flames that shot out of the clothing as it burned. They covered themselves with Vaseline in order to protect themselves from chafing during the long wait. They felt connected to one another by their dry coughs. As they got thinner, the tendons in their necks would jut out grotesquely whenever they swallowed.

38. On the morning they died, they glued themselves together by their genitals, collapsed on the bed, and began eating each other's faces. The boy and the girl expired with a tiny mutual spasm as a brilliant pink light flooded the room.

KEN AND KATHY

Did you know Ken and his wife Kathy had some twins?
Did you know Kathy and her husband Ken had some twins?
They had twins!
You know him
and his wife Kathy?
Well, they had some twins!
Did you know her
and her husband Ken
Had some twins?

Did you know him, Ken
and her, Kathy?
Well they had some twins!

They had twins!
Kathy and Ken had twins!

Him
and
his
wife
Kathy...

She
and
her
husband
Ken...

He
and
his
wife

Kathy...

Her
and
her
husband
Ken...

Well, get this:
They had twins!
Yes they did...
They had twins!

You know Kathy and Ken?
Well, they had some twins!

He and his wife Kathy
and she and her husband Ken...
Well, they had some twins!

Do you know her?
Do you know him?
Well, Ken and Kathy had some twins!

Kathy and her husband Ken
and Ken and his wife Kathy
had some twins!

They had some twins!
They went and had themselves some twins!
Oh yeah, they're gonna have their hands full with those twins
because Ken and Kathy
just had twins!

Him, and his wife Kathy
and she and her husband Ken...
Get...
Get them on the other end...
Get...

Get those twins on the other end.
Get...
Get Ken and Kathy's twins in here.
They had twins!

NOTES HOME

For Justin

1.

You have been bad-I will have to beat your punk ass.

2.

You are an extremely unruly person-I will have to pound your
punk head on the desk.

3.

You are not even aware of your influence over other people-
please see me after class.

4.

You should learn to pay attention-someday you may be hit by a
car and I'll be the punk driving it.

ANGELS

Angels with migraines
Spinning angels on cakes
Angels on baby
Clothing, trees,
Zap
The angels
Chubby angels
Los Angeles
Fuck you
When angels have migraines
Their hair is set ablaze
And they go into convulsions
Freaking
Peaking
They smell
Of zero ozone
Sulfur
Fuck you
They poke up
Through the clouds and say
"I'm a tree
I have green hair
I'm over here
No, I'm over there"
Angels with egg on their face
Angels picking at St. Francis' teeth
Angels in neon blue rayon
Angels driving forklifts
Moving meat
Across a yellow brick road
Angels in my popcorn
Telling me what to do in the movie
Angels in pain

With major migraines
Feign grief
And fan themselves nonchalantly
Angels banging their headaches
Against the wall motherfucker
Angels with tiny silver guns
And angels with torches
And angels with video cameras
Trying to get a headache on tape
And angels eating hamburgers
And angels dousing their wings with gasoline
And setting them on fire
And angels with vomit around their cherubic smiles
And angels who implore you to ignore them
As they pound their heads on the rocks
Hoping you'll get a migraine too.

JACKASS

"Ah ha, I thought so, a total jackass!" exclaimed the attending physician who was performing an autopsy on the dead man who lay strapped to a chrome gurney. He made an incision from the neck to the pubis and what was revealed just under his skin was the hide of a total jackass.

GOTHAM SELECTRIC MINIATURES

1.
BALZAC PERSON
The main Balzac person is off today.

2.
WORMY BODY
A padded bra won't help a wormy body.

3.
SHAKESPEARE
The Shakespeare section is behind the counter.

4.
DIAMOND DISTRICT
Here we all are in the heart of the diamond district.

5.
CHILDPROOF CAP
No one should play table hockey with one of these.

6.
BALLPARK IDEA
I brought these little monsters along because I didn't want to bring anything too heavy.

7.
GREAT WORD
Audit.

8.
BLACK PHLEGM
Guess what I have in my hands?

9.
HIRED MATHEMATICS
The drone of midtown delights me.

10.
JUST A BIT OF HONEY
On my buttercup.

GODS FIGHT WITH PINK FISTS

The blind fists of God.
The glass fists of God.
The ruby neck of God.
The blood splattered ribs of God.
The Lincoln Center magnitude of God.
The fiery chunks of God's pink ass.
The lovely swirl of God's gorgeous thighs.
The odd curl of God's marble wrist.
The Day-Glo hue of God's vitamin piss.
The all out hot fuck of God.
The smeared mouth of God's self-portrait.
The loud bang of the snubbed-nosed God.
The deep thud of God's dark green jeep.
The oven mitt hand-job of God.
The final abandonment of the threadbare God.
The creamy goo of God's glass eye.
The arrival of the unwanted God in the barn.
The pale wantonness of God's sexy throat.
The oddly shaped stain of God's presence in a tree fort.
The quivering belly of the fat ass God.
The vast and unbearable loneliness of God.
The steroid rage of the muscle God.
The enormous false eyelashes of God.
The bourgeois desire of the mega-mall God.
The chocolate fudge brownie map of God's rubber face.
The bible camp songs about God's purple Yankee.
The mother of pearl sprocket on God's chrome bike.
The complete gangly realism of God's peculiar fantasy.
The collapse of the pink-lunged God.
The deep-fried blue-eyed God.
The practical falsity of God's green acre.
Cruising with God in his gun metal gray fiberglass dune buggy.
The pink fists of God against God.
Somewhere on a beach there's a picture of two Gods
in a magazine under the heading:
GODS FIGHT WITH PINK FISTS.

PEACH PIT/BULLY PULPIT

It's quite possible that anxiety
could manifest itself as a pit in your stomach.
It could make you feel awkward
and glow awkwardly
and turn silver and orange and yellow too.

After a month or two of this
guilt will inevitably set in
and panic too
and your heart will become swollen
as a beefsteak tomato.

You'll start to look ashen and complex.
You'll forget to wash your hands after you poop.
You'll shake hands with filthy strangers
and then you'll sit down to eat enormous feasts
with those very same hands.
You'll become totally unconcerned with germs
while the hyper-golden antibacterial soap
sits unused above your dirty bathroom sink.

You'll soon learn that it's a law of physics
that if you walk backwards with a camera
you won't be able to see where the fuck you're going.
You'll also learn that people simply do not
like being struck on the head by sharp pieces of metal.

You'll start to feel that you've found a certain
poise amid the turmoil.
You'll stroll through life like a graduate
of the Fred Astaire School of Ass Dancing.
But all this time you'll become worse
than anyone could expect you to be.

You'll juggle drops of your own blood—
You'll fuck down and dive
into milk and sugar and snow—
You'll feel the positive charge of negativity
like a glass of something strong and dangerous.

When you try to sleep
A yucky old man will shine one hundred flashlights
into your sorry yellow eyeballs.
You'll go down to the New Age Store and buy candles
scented with citrus and spice.
You'll take to wearing a little vest made of nylon
and stuffed with triple fat goose down.
You'll wake up one morning to find
yourself sliding down a snow covered hill.
You'll wave your hands in the air above your head
as though you've been inadvertently set on fire.
You'll feel your ass become red and chapped.
You'll want to establish contact with total strangers.
You'll feel a wetness on the back of your head
and it will take awhile for you to realize that you've been shot
by someone you pissed off years ago.

At that very moment
there will be a huge CHORAL FLAIR
and you'll laugh your last laugh
laughing loudly as lamp-lit light lifts
lights lamping loud laughs looking lovely
losing your shirt, your shoes, and your keys.

You'll stumble into an Italian restaurant
wearing only a blood-soaked down vest.
You'll sit down at the table
covered by a red and white checkered tablecloth
and order chocolate pasta from the startled waiter.
You'll motion for him to come closer
come closer, come closer, come closer...
and you'll whisper into his filthy, wax coated ear:
"18 grams of fat baby, 18 grams of fat...."

MIRACLE CONFERENCE

When she sang everyone had to do deep knee bends
or look deeply occupied in a newfangled high-end
        calisthenics routine.
A white sink full of gray water.
Where can we establish a deep knee bender?
The gray silk scarf is soaking in the sink.
She sings about my hands as she bathes in the gray river.
At the Miracle Conference she stepped up to the microphone
in the roped off area for questioners
and sang the words "his hands are lovely"
The words she sang made the delegates go wild.
I went running head first into a newfangled sink of water
in front of the police officer.
My head sank into a soundless deep knee bend
while I wiped my nipples with the gray silk.
As the police officer watched me he mopped his brow
with an ordinary gray kitchen sponge.
I pulled a fish from the sink and threw it into
        the river of gray sponges.
High energy deep knee bender?
The words she sang made the police officer go wild.
She sang of gray sponges in a river lined with barking dogs.
She sang about my gray hands.
She sang about the gray river.
She sang about the bright gray days.
The light is so harsh it's squeezing the life out of my animals.
The police officer sang in a laid back manner
        as he drove the cruiser.
He told me realism requires great patience as he wrapped
An old street map around a vanilla-scented votive candle.
I am in the cruiser with the police officer,
and he's rubbing my left thigh as he drives.
I tossed a sponge out the window of the cruiser into the river of

gray sponges.
I may be squeezing the life out of my animals.
She stands in a roped-off area and sings about my hands.
The police officer seems uninformed and distant.
A bright gray flash lights up the interior of the car for an instant.
I may have been pouring gasoline into a funnel
or squeezing the life out of my animals.
When the bed gets damp she stops singing.
I am driving you to the gray river.
The police officer wrapped a vanilla scented votive candle
in an old street map and stuffed it in my mouth.
I am squeezing the life out of my animals.

THE INCIDENTS

The grill is lifted a bit at one end and rolled a few feet across the yard. Pale insects scurry about in the ruts left behind. Before wrapping the wound with a bandage, Gatorade is poured over it. The plastic suicide kit contains some needles, a razorblade, and several black pills with white skulls on them. Memories of licking aspirin tablets. The metallic mint taste of envelope glue. A loud pop is heard and suddenly a row of gigantic Klieg lights illuminate the once dark parking lot. A half-dozen or so locals have stopped by to watch the spectacle of lights. A man in a pale green golf shirt arrives and several people begin snapping pictures of him sashaying across the parking lot. After an hour or so everyone packs up and leaves.

A small pond in the middle of a field covered by a huge sheet of tin foil. It sparkles and glares under the headlights of a car pulling up out of the darkness.

In town there is an overly emotional gift giving sequence where people shriek with delight and embrace one another whenever a package is ripped open and its contents displayed. One man receives a box of red soil in an amber tinted glass box. He becomes so ecstatic when he opens the gift that blood comes out of his nose. He feels the blood on his lip and discreetly wipes it away with a greasy napkin. A short while later they find the man collapsed next to the grill. Charred T-bone steaks give off a thick smoke. The dirt at the bottom of the inflatable baby pool is stirred up by the cop's black Oxfords. He curses the placement of the pool and makes his way towards the side of the house. A red bow skids across the driveway and lodges next to a rusty sprinkler. A piece of cellophane from a snack cake flutters on an old wooden picnic table. The man bleeding from his nose lies next to the smoking grill. Under the tree, next to the pond, a white dog lies panting.

While getting a mandatory physical at the police academy they had asked him a rather peculiar question to which he answered no less peculiarly:

Not much has ever come out of me, but when it did it was brown, tan, red, and occasionally clear and colorless. I must not forget varying hues of yellow. Very few primary colors come out of me. White is not a color, per se, but it has come out of me in a lot of different shades over the years. My body was born in a sun chariot covered with tin foil.

By the time the cop found him, some of the blood around his mouth was dry and flaky.

Months later pictures of the man in the pale green golf shirt appeared in a clothing catalogue but no one could tell that he was standing in a parking lot.

All the taboos have been broken with varying degrees of success. Yet we are still moved when we hear a thorny little lullaby. Ditto for tomorrow. It made life easier the first few months. After a year or so it got just plain rugged.

A white dog lies panting under a tree.

In the car a group of boys play heavy metal music and thrash about, slamming their backs against the seat and snapping their heads forward to the beat. The sky looks milky under the pale moonlight. The car's headlights shine in the dog's eyes and they glow ominously back at the car but the boys don't notice because they're lost in the music. Pink dolphin of dog rises between its legs.

As the ambulance pulled away with the man's body inside, the guests sullenly shuffled about, absently picking up gifts that had made them deliriously happy only a few hours before.

The boy behind the wheel of the car has to buff it with a chamois to keep the original copper hue. He also uses a special waxy copper cleaning solution, an old rag for detail areas, and a high velocity spraying hose. He refers to these items as his "arsenal."

The boys in the car are smoking pot and yelling over the loud music. One can hear repeated references to "city" and "pussy." There is a gunshot and suddenly one of the boys emerges from the rear passenger door and staggers towards the pond. Black silhouette of the boy with the copper car's headlights illuminating him from behind.

A few miles away there are some people just getting up and others just going to bed. A box of red dirt next to a grill. A boy and a girl lay in the high grass next to the pond. They are unaware of the dampness of the ground or the green insects scurrying around an open can of beer. She is rubbing his cock and he is moaning. Her shirt is off though he never says her name. His name is Chuck because she says it loud enough that the white dog's ears perk up from across the pond.

Because the gunshot wound has pierced a major artery near the boy's heart, he is having trouble navigating his way towards the pond. He doesn't hear a girl yell "Chuck!"

The sound of the gunshot is muffled enough by the loud music and the closed windows that the couple in the tall grass don't hear it. A boy staggers to the pond and lands face first against the tin foil covering the water. The weight of his body rips the foil and he sinks into the pond.

The copper car's headlights illuminate the white dog. "I'm coming, look at me!" exclaims the boy in the tall grass. The music in the car stops. Crickets. The dog barks. A cop gets in his cruiser, reaches under the seat, sighs, and takes a swig of red cough syrup directly from the bottle. The copper-hued car starts with a roar and speeds away, spitting gravel and dust in its wake. Startled by the commotion, the girl rushes to put her shirt back on. The dog licks between its legs in the darkness.

THE SPEED OF LIGHT: A MESSAGE

They've managed to slow down the speed of light so that when I turn on my lamp to read a book the light moves out of the lamp like chilled honey. It oozes slowly across my chest, arms, hands, and finally: my book in real time. What I find more disconcerting is that even my reading comprehension has slowed down with the light. I can't help but think it also has something to do with this gas in the air.

The chain around my bike is actually a gas, or so the people who've slowed down the speed of light would like me to believe.

I've been tracing the outline of your mouth in the space you've left behind. As you walked down the street I stood behind you and thought "your mouth has touched this gas, it might have been in your lungs." So we may still be breathing the same slow gas.

I've become so fatigued that I can't confirm anything but this gas and the slowness of light in here.

I mention the gas not so much to frighten you as to make you aware that it has less to do with the cars that pass on the express-way near here than it does with this new grayness entering my field of vision on each side. I'll refer to it as "the fog" in order to sim-plify things, though it is a fog only I can see. Please don't join me at the restaurant if you see me, pretend we've never met, it will be better that way and it will allow me to avoid the confusion of try-ing to remember your name.

I will be eating eggs that are scrambled though you should not take note of this because you will be walking by as though you are not aware of my presence in the room. However, you may see me twitch in an almost imperceptible manner. This will be a coded "hello" that you should not respond to.

The rest will be entirely up to you (after you've left the restaurant and are safely inside the van you may wish to write down your impressions, taking special notice of your pulse, your breathing rates and the time of your last intake of food). By measuring your blood sugar at this point you will get a fairly accurate picture of your mood should it be fluctuating as you sit in the van gathering yourself.

In summation, I am looking forward to a nice vacation with many more seemingly chance encounters as the one mentioned above. Remember, it is very important to keep a logbook or journal of each encounter. Never go overboard with the descriptions but simply write down your direct observations. Emotions (written down) have a tendency to betray us in later years, just a hint.

TOWERS OF MY APPRECIATION

I had thoughts that came alive while looking out the window. A lot of things with apples in them. Apple tarts, for instance. A quart of milk is like looking at the enemy that just so happens to be a machine I can't quite get the knack of. I can't operate it. The rule of air currents popularizes the concept of a marble at the base of the brain. Any brain will do, man or beast. This is the product of the environment blared out a window at some police officers.

A casual handshake in a corner creates a symphony of flash pot bulbs. A whole evening is like that. A minute later and it all comes flashing back to me during an electrical storm. Snuff Films. We called you "The Champion" but we meant to call you "The Onion." The phone rings in a hut by the pool, you are there. A wet tissue that smells of chlorine sits by the lip of the pool. Today you are "The Champion" but tomorrow you will be "The Onion."

My body is dissolving in the afternoon light. On a table, in pain. At the base of my brain there is a marble. Two men on bicycles ride through an area of Brooklyn known as "Red Hook." Green cup fantasy booth come alive in the jellied light of clouded noon. "Looking good in Brooklyn." A hand-me-down is like a label you can only read under a special light. Cobalt blue glass ashtray. One million quarts of money arrive in special paper containers which crowd the dock until we get there. The great millions go around the block in a special car.

The Coppertone is leaking onto my fur. Now my hands and fur are greasy. Spread-eagled on the dock, he meditates. A glass sits next to him full of brown liquid. My neck muscles get tense and my movements become jittery as I read the cryptic codes. The day is festooned with the fleshy limbs of animals.

I am a water breather so I can go on like that forever. I brought a camera because I'm a mood swinger. A lot of this stuff is coming your way too. In the mirror your nose is blurred because you have a sinus infection. Silver scratched by a blue diamond: "The Onion."

My arms are neglected but not disposed of just yet. Explosives dissolve in Sprite. A cup next to fish with raw, gaping sores. The fish are fizzing. Reading chunky light like words. My hands make words like a shadow comes to bed. Slits gap wrist and shoots juice to wild ones. Waving goodbye to the astronaut as well as the submariner. A man pisses off the side of the dock and comes back with his lungs in a cup. Now everything is fizzing.

He says he puts them in a blender and then injects them into his veins. A cobalt blue syringe. Braun Utensils. The fit of the tiny teeth chewing roses. My mask runneth over. Everything is rough and grainy. Other green flowers in transit all the way to Amanita. Sent for and came.

THE CANDY

Whenever the desire for candy got to be too much for her, her hands would pop off and from out of the stems would shoot all varieties of delicious candy. After her desire for candy was sated she knew how to tie her hands back on without any hands connected to her arms. It wasn't a trick, it was a skill that she had perfected on her own, for others on planet earth had lost this skill long ago. But she had not lost her desire for candy.

She imagined the bubbling fizz of Pop Rocks under her tongue which would bring forth a soft contentment to all her frazzled senses. She burned incense and thought she was a hippie. She had a macho boyfriend with long stringy blond hair and a face that looked like a flank steak which she would leap into like a starving ferret each night at the merest provocation.

To hell with your Christmas pudding, what Santa needs is a cigarette.

She got a deep macho Santa massage from her daydream hippie Santa that transformed her bones into dust in which little insect children would play with their insect candy and bring it back to their nest where they would all eventually die.

The visions pleased her. She wished she could melt inside her thoughts and mix them with Jell-O and rich chocolate milk and death and little piglets and Christmas cookies and all the stories her Mother told her while she was growing up. She changed the outcome of each one to make it seem as though she weren't the one getting the autopsy in the diner. No, it was her Mother flayed open on the condiment table near the kitchen and this made her happy. Whenever she thought of this her brain would swell up and force its way into her cheeks making her look puffy and delirious. But all this changed, for she became a scary bad man. Bad. A very bad man.

In a moment of dreamy weakness she allowed herself to disappear. Zing. Hazing. Out of life only for an instant, she opened her eyes: "It's okay. I'm back in life. Everything is okay."

She hoped to see creamy blue skinned boys with orchids sewn into their silver hair swinging languidly on hammocks like some dopey Yes album cover. But no, instead of transforming into something beautiful, she came back as my Uncle Jackie, the fat guy that smoked all the cheap cigars and let all the ashes fall on his belly, burning through his hazy gray shirt. The polyester scum-bucket. Uncle Jackie: the guy who used to touch me on the leg and make me feel really uncomfortable when I sat on his lap. She came back as him. And she came into my house and said: "I'm your Uncle Jackie now and I want to talk to you and I want to touch your thigh and make you feel really uncomfortable. I want to make you feel really bad."

She was in the alternative universe of chemical substances. Her synapses were snapping at each other like wild hogs. So she locked them all in one room and obscured them with a light gauzy curtain which she back-lit with black light because she felt groovy as the pale yellow power burst up her spine. She knew she was walking everywhere with nowhere to go, nowhere to run, nowhere to hide. All the molecules in her surging body ending on the horizon of an unending sky. She felt her warm urine running down her pale thighs. She felt everything trembling as she vomited her last meal of apple candy.

Emptied, she shuddered, sat up and said, "I've had a hard day, death no longer frightens me." For she knew life and she knew that life was nothing more than a secure foothold in absolutely nothing. But she clung to it desperately because she had no hope, no life, no future, and her macho boyfriend was pounding on the door because she'd been burning incense so she could mellow out and he doesn't like his work clothes to smell like sandalwood or any of those hippie things.

At that very moment she looked in the mirror and traced the outline of her face with her index finger. She saw the lines deepening and becoming more pronounced. With each passing moment she was getting older. To hell with the peaches and cream complexion.

What she needed was the taste of fuzz. So she pulled an old Santa beard from a beat up hatbox. The beard reminded her of an aging hippie's hair. She curled on the floor, placed the beard under her head, and drifted peacefully off to sleep.

DEAR, I LOVE

My symptoms have become bizarre. As the silver liquid is drained from my lungs so the super-charged music implies nobility. Our system is completely refined. Think of the names of things but don't use those words to describe the names. Think of the animals as expensive white go-go boots like a wrestler's shoes.

People are walking around...and seeing things...what words are for...to describe what the people are doing. I can't write about them without breaking the crayon.

My skin is leaking bright yellow smoke. A drawing of a stressed out animal on the wall. The soprano comes in. "Oh goodie," I think. Little arguments break out on the edge of my seat. Smiling broadly...my entire mouth stretched across my face...so that I'm all mouth now, where my face used to be. I scream with skinny delight.

Sadness...scooping out my brain with a common wooden spoon. Sticking a drill in my forehead and turning into the crybaby Frankenstein. The words, the distance, the planet of stars, where everyone on it is famous...movie stars as the only important people. A solemn moment that I digress...I weep fruity pebbles. If you were the dog I'd walk you straight to hell so I could get these dried spiders out of my blood.

The trembling I do now slipping into the cool blue water. Soaking in the memory on the veranda...wake up coffee...before that, a swim in the ocean with friends...a room...startled into submission...my slowness...the hands of the clock are flowers...blooming slower and slower...giving me time to brace myself for midnight...making no provisions for the flesh.

Let us not stop saving ourselves from these days that weigh us down. The brown door. Blue and brown books. The money is all gone. A mouth full of brown sugar. The sweet language of screams. Memory is cheap. I broke the crayon.

Dear, I love

ALIEN LEMON EGG

Some people had a dream about me so they cut the back of my arm. It smelled like freshly cut lemons. My arm sprayed lemon juice when it was sliced by the scalpel. Someone was having a dream about me because they were reminded of something I left behind on a table long ago and they were just now running across it in some room in their dream. So I landed face first on the concrete when they cut the back of my arm. It was the inside of a lemon on the street in my head. There was yellow pulp on the street where I landed because someone had thrown a rotten lemon at a parade that had gone by a few hours before.

Take a normal steak. If you dream of a place you actually were with another person then chances are that person will eventually connect wire electrodes to a piece of meat. Pinch the meat with pinchers. Like something a lobster has, only with wires attached. Like jumper cables in a leather chair on nipples. Like a car battery with clothespins on the connectors. Without a leather chair at least lead fittings on the front of my shirt. You are probably not more than five or six miles away from a person you have a dream about. Statistically at least, what sort of current dies and comes to life again?

They squeezed my index finger in order to get a sample of the juice from that part of my body. If you hold an image in your mind of a person's face while you masturbate it will be just like fucking that person. You might have met that person at a sales conference or a family gathering or in the basement of a church. Keep poking around. They pressed hard and out from under my fingernail popped a lemon seed. It bounced to the pavement, rolled in the dirt on the side of the road and disappeared.

If a steak were given enough attention or television coverage, it would, under certain specific circumstances, defuse the will to live in a majority of the people who saw it on the television. You might want to start your own group of dream friends who will look out for you to make sure you don't have a dream that the steak is decomposing on the television. You may want to pack it in ice the next time you think or dream of it. Wire electrodes pinching the meat as they peeled a freshly picked lemon from a tree.

It was no longer an ordinary lemon. It looked more like an alien lemon egg. Your friends should take care of you should you ever need their help. You might want to break the ice with some of them now.

The meat would flop around from the electricity running through it. It would even start to cook where the wire electrodes were attached. This goes to show you that all it takes to imply that you are friendly is to shake hands with everyone in the room. If you ever find yourself dreaming you're in a room full of strangers make an effort to shake hands with everyone in the room. You never know who you could be dreaming about. Perhaps one of the people you're dreaming about could give you help when you really need it. The meat might actually start to cook where the wire electrodes are attached. If you can't hold an image of the meat and the electrodes in your mind's eye then it might be a good idea to break the ice with some of the people standing around the periphery of the dream. Small groups are best. From the seed: a tree. When I landed on the concrete what? You might have had sex with that person at a sales conference or the basement of a church or some other social gathering. It must have been some sort of lemon egg. We picked one just to see. Go introduce yourself to those people in the corner, they were just looking over here.

I thought I could relax when I fell asleep but everyone knows this is not true. I was penniless then and I never met any rich people so I started having random dreams in chaotic flashes and pops. A bit of foresight like an old scratched-up record. I was making friends with rich people so I could relax in crowded rooms. Some of my poor friends are even rich now. What did I do? I got a nice place to stay that was nicer than the place I'd been which was a dump. At one party I opened a packet of sugar and poured it onto an old vinyl record that was playing on the turn table. It was like going back in time. Old trombone jazz.

*

One of my jobs during the summer months was emptying water drippings from an air conditioner that collected in a bucket outside a health club. It was a boring job so I took to realizing things in order to pass the time.

I realized that everything on the face of the earth could be transformed into a fine dust that could then be inhaled in order to get a mild, heady buzz.

My heart hurt because I felt a sudden sadness begin at my feet (I had a knack for locating emotions in my body parts) and move up through my legs and into my sternum where it sat firmly and refused to budge for what seemed an eternity I just sort of stood there rocking back and forth with that pain in my chest as I waited for the bucket to fill up.

Everything glowed with a mysterious yellow electricity.

When the deli owner absently dropped change onto the back of my hand I felt that electricity. When I felt the pressure on my chest it was because someone had punched me at that exact spot on my chest.

I stuck out my hand with the palm down and the deli owner hesitated an instant before dropping four pennies onto the back of it. The coins bounced off my knuckles and onto the floor. I saw the electricity in the coins as they rolled in steady circles around my feet.

Pink Chinese menu blowing down the street.

I felt a bony fist strike the side of my face. Not sure if the wet tingle was blood or water, I reached up to touch my cheek. It was blood. I fiddled around in the wound with my index finger and realized that if I stuck it in at an angle I could massage my cheek bone.

Bright copper coins swirled around my feet.

I made a mental note of the music that I heard playing. It was cool, calm, and one might even say downright soothing. I could hear the music better by laying down on the sidewalk. This wasn't at all like the aftermath of falling from a retaining wall when I'd had my breath knocked out. This was more like a pleasant relaxed state that made it easier to have intense reveries.

*

Strange people under green florescent lights. Like some geekfest of lonely poetmen who need something to do so they all masturbate into socks and dream of the holy vagina mother in a flannel nightgown of mama blow-job while daddy works the nightshift (hot bird tongue of mama under green light in the bell tower glass-topped air shaft). Hot buttered tongue of the mommy stick. The poetmen are moaning in ecstasy on the melted plastic cushions over a silver radiator. Fumes of fuck sauce. Hot lips touch melting hot chocolate drops on wax cock...

The oddity of the men-deformed under the light-they fuck the mama- and the mama, large, with three vaginas says "Oh yes!" and "Good Fuck-job!"

One of the men in sexual ecstasy blurts out "Call me mama!" At which point the action stops. The men lose their erections and make faint whimpering sounds as the mama glares at the man who wants to be called "mama." Silence. The mama flings the men off her except for the "mama man." She tosses him violently onto his back and sticks her hand into his mouth while calling him "mama" very gently... "mama...mama..." almost as though it's a question: "mama?" The mama man's eyes close as she plays with his cock with her free hand. He moans as she sticks her whole hand violently into his mouth—deeper—he gasps—she reaches into his throat—deeper—he deep-throats her hand—she wiggles her fingers in his windpipe—he can't breathe but he barely struggles as he turns blue—his cock goes soft—tension leaves his body—she pulls her hand out of his mouth—it's covered with grayish- green mucous—she flings it into the air and it lands with a wet slap against the wall—she takes the same hand with the remnants of mucous on it and rubs it on her vagina while reaching around madly for other cocks on the freakish men all huddled in the corners—she rubs them wildly as she watches the mucous ooze down the wall—the mama man lies blue on the floor with fuck sauce drying on his belly.

There is calm again after the mama gives hand-jobs to the remaining men. They collapse in helium release mode where they languidly fill bag-gies full of raspberry jelly—the jelly sizzles and raspberry seeds crackle as they toss the baggies onto the radiator. They nod under the narcotic smell of burnt sugar and dream of spitting into an ancient hand during a frantic hand-job in the back of a cab as the lights of the city flash by.

∗

The scent of lemons.

IF GOD LIVES INSIDE OF US

If god lives inside of us
it's almost worth having him come over.
Like grandma says:
"I hope he likes peanut butter and jelly
so I can enjoy watching him leave."
What am I supposed to do for a pillow tonight?
It's almost a nightmare watching him leave
with my peanut butter and jelly sandwich.
If god lives inside of us
I hope he likes what I'm doing for a pillow
so I can enjoy peanut butter and jelly.
Well, it's almost worth watching him inside of us
but what am I supposed to do for a pillow tonight?
I can enjoy watching him leave.
Like grandma says, "what am I supposed to do?"
If he likes peanut butter and jelly for a pillow
I can enjoy watching him come over tonight.
If god lives inside of us what am I
supposed to do for peanut butter and jelly tonight?
Watching him leave for a pillow
so I can enjoy watching him leave.
If god lives inside of us, like grandma says,
"what am I supposed to do for a pillow tonight?"
I hope he likes peanut butter and jelly.
It's almost worth having him come over
just so I can enjoy watching him leave.
If god likes peanut butter and jelly
what am I supposed to do for a pillow?

VOID WHERE PROHIBITED BY LAW

I want you to have some of what I'm having
Which is why I've painted you into the cauliflower.
This place is a wreck—
I can't even find what I was going to give you in the first place.
My gimmick is spraying pudding from a Super Soaker
So I'll need you to duck when you see me loading it.
Bring the chicken kebob in here
So I can scrub your back with it.
In about a crocodile we'll have other guests
Dropping by who are known for their "Frenzied Acts."
We just love their beautiful palsied arms akimbo.
Just in case they don't show up
We can screw one of the replicants I made instead.
If we can't get our sexy parts to match one of the replicant's
We might need to take out a piece of your stomach
And attach it to your leader's shoulder. Be forewarned:
The entire procedure might be seen on national television.
You could have so much more
If you would just worship me like you worship Satan.
This is a secret message that means:
We may have to kill you both (and eat you)
Or at least one of you.
Trot in on the horse you diagnosed on the web.
In case of fire boil this message.
This is your password, I'll be your guide.
You rode in on me.

THINK EIGHT

Walk on by how much you were undone
by all who came before you or
who have read of your use.
So I can carry you—
your lightness
to the place where some of us are funny
and many of us are huge.
Setting your body down on the straw
and propping a rock under your head
and not even wanting to crush it
there on the straw, your head.
We will be able to sit there and become awake
but not too much
because everything is still wonderful
when you're half-awake.
Why do you sleep so much anyway?
My warm arm made you laugh a red laugh.
She, together with them
knew us only when we were sad at it.
Doomed, they were all once pretty.
They told us what to eat,
how to act, and who to be
for maximum earning potential.
No live jumps over canyons,
or olive groves to spruce up.
I worked hard on this month.
I even ran down there and got us
a fir tree and put it in the yard.
I played yes and even came without holdouts
because that time around it was me in the crowd.
Are you even listening?
Would it be better if that's what it was all about: "listening?"
Hot clean lark came just after the storm.

I found a note and let out a tiny cry
cut smaller from a bout with the scissors.
I hope these days go well for you,
today for you, and some for myself.
Old light is nearer the speed of light when it's long gone.
When we say "the speed of light"
what we mean is
we could break it by then
and we did.

SHE WAS RED

She was really red.
She was red.
She was really well read.
She was red.
She was well, red.
She was red, she was red, she was red, she was red,
She was really well read.
Red all over.
Red on top.
Red in the middle.
Red on the bottom.
She was red.

She was Cincinnati red.
She was a communist.
She was Warren Beatty red.
Damn red.
Extra large red.
She was post-punk red.
Red Lord.
Hawaii five red.
Gilligan's red.
She was The President of Red.

Question:
What's black and white and red all over?
Answer:
She, that's who.

The early bird catches the red.
A stitch in time saves red.
Walking on water was built on red.

Question:
Which came first: the chicken or the red?
Answer:
She did, because she was born red.

She was a Boston Red Sock.
She was Johnnie Walker Red.
She was cherry red.
She was candy apple red.
She was the red lobster.
She was Marlboro red.
She was Red Buttons.
She was Red Skelton.
She was Redd Foxx.

Question:
Why did the chicken cross the red?
Answer:
To get to her because she was well read.

She was blood red.
She was beet red.
She was Good Old Ruby Red Dress.
She was red at night sailor's delight.
She was red in the morning sailors take warning.
She was the red-nosed reindeer.
She was Marquis de Red.
She was a red wine cooler.
She was a red eye flight.
She was Satan red.
She was pomegranate red.
She was red alert.
She was read up on everything.

Ready or not she's really well read.
She was red.
She was well read.
She was really well read.

THE INDUSTRY STANDARD

In the new house of glamorous impositions we paid for a good time with our windfall and it was simple: a 17-pound meal actually ended up being more like a 100-pound snack. But we paid as we grew, and boy did we grow. We spent a load of dough on the corporate eaters, wheelers, and dealers. We shelled out big bucks for high-end Kobe beef business lunches that were frequently known to end in a headlock or two.

As you well know, the power of prominence has a special bloated charm that tends to exacerbate as well as dishevel a person, heck, some might even say it destroys the soul, but that might be overstating the matter. To no it's just business.

It's a fact that most industrial men and women prefer to be plastered abroad (or at least gorge themselves on the native cuisine). They like to remain open with their affections while maintaining the ability to discriminate between winners and losers.

Let me get to the point: sit with me, and connect with me. Take my pulse if you feel so inclined, and then we can slip out behind those expensive red velvet curtains.

I'm writing to you from a rocket ship, I'm writing to you in a pair of commanding Frye Boots. Did you mistake me for someone else? Think about the time you work and worry, and the fact that you do a lot of thinking while you worry, so worry it up, as long as you get the work done. You have an uncanny ability to think more than actually pleases us here, but don't make it a habit, that would be unfounded and potentially wound-inducing. There's room for you at the top, but not too much. Good luck.

I WAS ABLE OR MY LIFE AS I RECALL IT

1

When I came here I was braining and I was handheld. I was making Crater Music for the New City and then it got to the point where there were Wildcats and Compressed Gas and that brought me together.

I painted my greatest session who was an inspiration to start my collection. When I came here I brought something. I went to the New City with a Bible Phone because I listened to Tally Grips and More Chex.

Anyhow, this is how I came here. In the first scene I was the instigator in the slumps and my direction of dreaming was: I Can. I was able was My Concept.

Sometimes there was blood all over The Campers who came from The Outer Banks just to see the brass section I'd sketched out on a napkin, framed, and hung on a wall in The Communal Cabin. My Work was said to have Value because it met a Certain Need so it became Valuable. Among The Campers who crowded into The Cabin was a Little Girl who was hugging a Dead Squirrel. There was Blood all over her Yellow Dress and her hands were shaking-making The Squirrel's head bounce around a lot and spill more blood on her dress- it was quite serious.

This Little Girl became My Daughter and later My Wife through a series of Coincidences. When the Market of Needs bottomed-out I became a plasterer; applying plaster and stucco to Mobile Homes. But all this time I was humming My Music in my head and when I got home at night I would cry into the tape recorder which was pretty sad and funny when I look back on it from the vantage point of Worldwide Success. The tapes just came out like Warm Muffins. You'd love it if The Sounds came into Your House, I did and still do.

2

I edited The Golden Light for a few years. The Strange Thing was
I got beefy and jumpy when the light ceased to shine on any book
I picked up- which made The Enormous Collection less valuable
as time went by. I kept The Clippings in Shoeboxes in The Closet
and pulled them out from time to time after I'd eaten A Few
Sandwiches.

My Pig Paintings generally got compared to The Very Closed
Minds of Bad Ideas. It was like skating on Frozen Orange Juice.
The Pulp would always get me skidding on All Fours towards The
Great Wall. But it was only another of my many Minor Setbacks,
Close Calls and Character Flaws. I persisted- and in the end I had
nothing to show for it but a few King Crab Legs. When I sat down
to dinner I drowned my sorrows in Grape Juice and Bacon Strips.
This was my Fat Period, I'll admit- but one I learned from- for as
I got further away from my life- it seemed to be someone else's.

3

When the Leaves Died I did research into The Great History of
Needing which posed as a Grammar School filled with ordinary
forms like Pianos or Catholics. I wanted The Tunes to fall into the
Right Hands so I scraped by on Tuna and Chips for months at a
time, along with the ever-so-occasional Feast of Forgetting. I
learned that if you don't need something it's hard to attain the
American Dream so I set about discovering My Needs.

I don't have the information on The Time of Developing Needs
but I came closer to my Fellow Country People with Tacky
Handgrips and Soft Soap.

There was a pain in the Beige and it brought rain and the onset of
fever along with Jubilation and Shrieks from the sufferers of Mad
Flower Disease.

When I went electric, questions and comments came from all over the world. My theories on The Electricity of Needs were discussed on many a Web Page like The American Dream Page and The Questions and Comments Page.

This was the Birth Label Phase and I was not fading away anymore but doing a dance that seemed to be catching on with the New-Jackers who also liked their tuna rolled up in Whole Grain Tortillas. With My Reputation growing, I appeared on the Tarot Birthing Channel and The Universal Broadway Channel. I was just waiting around my house for the checks to come so I could go outside and cash them.

I did not know of the Yellow Rocks or The Corn Creeps but I fell into their trance on The Supreme Cornflakes of The Gemini Clan. There were rocks being smoked from genitals in the flinty mist while all kinds of juices were being guzzled from clay jugs. Many Serious Rides were taken into The Country of Moths where inhibitions seemed not to exist. In-flight calls were made in Desperation and Whispered into Ears on The Outer Banks where The Spells were not as Potent as those in the Motherland.

I new I'd hit bottom again when I woke up while making love to Sacred Tin Foil Suit. I found that by Smiling a lot I could become Form Fitting over time. I ate salads and bought Toothpaste and Cigarettes. I had High Velocity Fridays and Multiple Violence which never seemed to subside. My Skeleton Staff took Paramilitary Refuge Above the Law of Averages, which was only fitting due to My State.

4

Soon I was back on my feet, but they were not the feet I'd known before the Deluge, so My Thinking was as awkward as my Gait. At this point I became an Expert Swimmer and taught the Younger Ones: The Secret of Water Propulsion in Toxic Waters. This was The Summer of The Mosquito so the air was thick with Poisonous Gases which created an overall feeling of dizziness and ill-feelings towards The Leaders. I passed my days floating on my back in The Sludge but I grew tired of this and decided to test my ability to walk on The Land again. To my amazement I discovered that not only could I walk- but I could run without Bamboo Leg Shunts or Brass Leg Braces. I ran for hours at a time and thought of nothing but putting one foot in front of the other. My feats created Quite a Stir among The Neighbor People who contacted scouts from The Outer Banks who came to see me stretch my calves on the front steps and trot off in the direction of the Dead Highway.

I learned The Language of Celebrity and Fashion and took to wearing The Gucci. I forgot The Language of Pain and Disillusionment just as I forgot The Girl in the Yellow Dress hugging the Dead Squirrel. Mumbling The Language of Mumbles, I forked over hundreds of dollars for Bronze Badges and Air Goggles. This was my Green Period and the one I look back on with a certain Whimsical, if not Pompous, Nostalgia.

5

Without explanation I entered The Era of Disdain for My Peers. I felt nothing but revulsion for those among my people who were also Mining the Golden Vein of Needs. I found their company an Encumbrance to my own single-minded Purpose.

My clothes became tattered and I spent my days sleeping and my nights cursing The Ground Beneath Me. This was The Period where I thought I deserved a Reward for Standing Upright. I slept in the Arrestor Bed at the end of A Runway. I captured The Chemical in the breath of Oxen and Cattle and used it for ink to write down My Thoughts. I was on the verge of becoming The Angry Mystery Man Who Brings Death so I removed Seven Bags of Sand from my alimentary tract and became Truculent while Blooming Into Invisibility.

Suddenly there was this Drunk on The Runway who was Making Sex to The Vibraphone. I've never talked about it much, but I stayed together for two years because I could. It just goes to show you how easy it is to get people to compliment your good taste. I thought I could get My Message to The United States before The Revolution.

CUSH

MY MUSIC

My thigh bone
is actually a bell
and I ring it sometimes late at night.
I wait until everyone has gone to sleep
and then I tiptoe into the anteroom
sit down in my rocker
and pour myself a tall glass of Nyquil.
After I'm feeling drowsy from the medicine
I peel back the skin and muscle from my thigh
with a pair of cheap tweezers
from an old Operation game
and tap the bell inside
with a tiny brass
xylophone mallet.
This is my music.

A FREE FALL. NOTHING IS GLAMOROUS
ALL IS RESIDUAL IN THE DIZZY CARNIVAL
OF BIRD ALPO AND ELEPHANT MEMORY. CLIMB IT!
YEAH, LIKE CRAZY MAN, CRAZY.
I GOT RHYTHM COMEDY.
I GOT A BREAKER RIDER. FAT LIMBS. I GOT FAT
LIMBS.
I GOT A FAT ASS. I'M VACANT AND PLUMP.
I'M A MONSTER WITH CASH.
I'M A JERK WITH CHARM.
YOU THINK YOU'VE GOT ME PEGGED FOR CHARM?
WELL TRY CHURNING CREAM!
I'VE GOT A LITTLE LIQUID SMOKE PUMPED INTO
MY LUNGS....
FILL 'ER UP PAL! VINYL NIGHT
WITH STRAP ON MULCH. ROCK AND ROLL
AND DETACH THE WORM
FROM THE GLEAMING FOUNDATION.
BIRDS THROW SPARKS WHEN THEY HIT THE
GROUND.
KILL SONGS. DEVOUR ME YOU BIG STUPID CREEP.
NO BLADE STINK OR AQUAMARINE FOR ME. JUST
EVERGLADES AND ALLIGATORS.
PUNCH OUT MY LIGHTS DURING MY CURTAIN
CALL
BECAUSE I'M FULL OF MYSELF.
STICK A LIVE BUNNY IN MY STUPID MOUTH.
SPRITZ ME WITH GASOLINE ON A CROWDED SUB-
WAY TRAIN.
GEE, YOU'RE UPSET!
YOU SLAMMED THE CUPBOARD DOOR SHUT.
YOU THINK OPERA IS FOR JERKS. WELL GOD
DAMN.
WHY DON'T YOU STUFF GRAPES IN MY NOSTRILS?
WHY DON'T WE GET ON THE CARNIVAL RIDE

OF YOUR MOOD SWINGS?
NEXT TIME WE'LL PLAY FREEZE TAG IN THE MEAT
COOLER FOR REAL.

IMPERIAL CROWN

Hey, you've got eyes
like nobody else I know!
I'm only kidding....
I think it's sweet
the way the weather
feels like skin mischief down here
(it sort of stings, actually).
When the F train
comes into the Second Avenue station
it raises dull skirts,
gloom dust and fright wigs
it ruffles yellow papers and blows
luminous rat poison
onto my imperial crown.
From now on it's just soot balloons,
purple pillars and human goo
and I like that too.

HOTEL VALIUM

it's so hot
I'm under an avalanche
of sinister cartwheeelers and
swift missives,
instead of sweet, deep kisses
to the back of the neck
heat kisses
I'll do anything
for that prickly feeling on my arms again

smelly rednecks bathe
in the memory you squandered
in the hope of finding peace

this is a vacant memorial
in honor of my misjudgment of you

what I really need right now
is to check into the hotel valium

I'm not sleepy
but my arm is asleep
and I haven't slept in three days
I'm tired but I can't fall asleep

you know
vicious people really suck

you're so fucked up
you always made a point of showing me
your favorite vein
go stare at your facility in the mirror
go wash yourself off

I took a shower
in the hotel valium
and instead of water
the blood of the lamb came out

I thought I'd checked
into the blood of the lamb hotel
but in the hotel valium
blood comes out of the spigot
and it's so hot.

SURPRISE

You can never be too sad if you head up into the blossoms
of love and torture. I'm here and there. A sad man hums
along to the radio song. The song is about wishes. He drinks
black coffee. He stirs his head into a frantic frenzy. He is
not ashamed of desire, but lives to tell the truth which is
not the same as being aware that something is changing;
that he dying. The sun is low across the sky. So long
December shadows. Tomorrow, dumped. Today, two white eyes.

PINEAPPLE, SANDALWOOD AND MARZIPAN

Someone is shouting at you
in a language you don't understand
but you don't care
because you've seen this movie before
and it's really funny
though it's terrible—the acting is stilted
and the editing is an abomination
according to Rex Reed.
This movie is your life!
You're on the silver screen
and you're soaring, you're magic
and your name is in corny little lights.
"Señor Mister" that's your new stage name!
And now you have it all:
pineapple, sandalwood and marzipan.
You spring to life at the mention of
"another fine restaurant."
You like being seen
even if it means looking at yourself—
So you check out your reflection
in shop windows, in mirrors, in car windows
as they rush past you, brushing your arm—
You're soaring, you'll never land,
you're just another bit of celluloid
for the Mamas and the Papas.

BOYS TOWN

for Newt

MOTHER FUCKER
FUCKER
SHITASS
ASSHOLE
COCK SUCKER
DIPSHIT
SHIT
TURD
SHIT HEAD
PILE OF SHIT
PRICK
HORSE'S ASS
PISS ANT
SON OF A BITCH
BASTARD
FUCK OFF
GO FUCK YOURSELF
SCREW YOU
UP YOUR ASS
UP YOURS
STICK IT (UP YOUR ASS)
CRAM IT
SHOVE IT
SUCK MY COCK
EAT ME
KISS MY ASS
DROP DEAD
BUZZ OFF
GET LOST
GO FLY A KITE
YOU DON'T KNOW JACK SHIT
YOU DON'T KNOW SHIT FROM SHINOLA

YOU DON'T KNOW YOUR ASS FROM A HOLE IN THE
GROUND
GO CHEW SOMEBODY'S ASS
GO RIDE SOMEBODY'S ASS
FLOG YOUR DONG
CANDY ASS
CHICKEN
YELLOW BELLY
WHAM BAM
BUNNY FUCK
TEAR OFF A PIECE OF ASS
RIDE TO PARADISE ON SOMEONE ELSE'S ASS
WHERE THE FUCK HAVE YOU BEEN ALL YOUR
LIFE?
GO GET IT FROM MISTER PALM AND HIS FIVE
SONS
KICK MY ASS FROM HELL TO BREAKFAST
YOU'RE WHACKING DOWN PEARS WITH YOUR
PRICK
YOU'RE A PRICK ON WHEELS
THEY SELL A LOT OF SHITTY JUNK TO TOURISTS
I'M GETTING THE FUCK OUT OF HERE FOR GOOD.

HOLLOW

Hollow is how I feel
you in the sunlight
dazzling in your majestic soda pop
shaking hands
with big shots
broken by degrees
you hum
and everything rumbles
with a subsonic purr.

It feels mysterious
getting jazzed up
and shiny for approximately
three minutes
but then
it's back
to gray ghoulish cloud clamps
and vacant mummy tunnels.

I can't breathe
I tried
but I'm
tired of breathing.

TWENTY SONGS FOR MY UNBORN FIFTH CHILD

I want to teach you how to leap over a fast moving car.
I want to teach you how to get stuck in a window
twenty floors up,
half in, half out.
I want to teach you how to write my name with chalk on the
sidewalk in front of your house.
I want to teach you how to smack my face when I'm bad.

OH THERE'S SO MUCH TO TEACH YOU.

I want to teach you how to drink a lot of coffee
and not freak out.
I want to teach you how to go to Coney Island all by yourself.
I want to teach you how to dump oatmeal on your Grandma's
bed.
I want to teach you how to load a gun with your teeth.

DO NOT PANIC.

I want to teach you how to get your penis caught
in a vacuum cleaner hose.
Can you turn on a faucet with your ass?
Well today I'm going to show you how.
I want to teach you all about horror and jubilation.
I want to teach you all about panic.

PLEASE DON'T PANIC YET.

I want to teach you how to tongue-kiss a priest
through the confessional screen.
I want to teach you how to joyously slap someone
on the back until their nose begins to bleed.
I want to teach you that a paper towel cylinder is not

a sex tool even if it's full of vaseline.
I want to teach you that a jackass shall not have a better
car than someone who is really popular.

LOOK AT ME WHEN I'M TEACHING YOU.

I want to teach you all about wonderful holiday rituals.
I want to teach you how to maintain a look of total surprise
as you vomit on your step-mother's lap.
I want to teach you how to stick a dead fish
in the ventilation system of your place of employment.
I want to teach you how to bob for fruit in a bucket of honey.

GET READY TO LEARN.

BUT

As you might have guessed
from the appearance of my name
on the shit list—
These are actual prayers
designed for an angry person
to use while addressing God.

But I have no use for those words.
I am performing another task,
in essence, I am composing my jackass prayer—
The one that gets me bonus points
for fine structure and elegant phrasing
in the face of calamity, like right now, fucker.

Punch this elegance on the mask.
This prayer is a vote of confidence in punishment.
Consider it a mandate for thrash and churn,
or something anxious and fidgety.

Consider calling all cars.
Consider stopping the game.
Consider a need other than sleep tonight.
Did I just say "sleep?"
I meant cops.

INSOMNIA

Here
among the evergreen jottings
of my well-pimpled lawns
rest busy bodies with
broken hands
and the old two, two,
two mints in one try
where we peel the losers like grapes
walking hand-in-hand
my eyes sting
they're so blue they're green
my eyes are peeled
I get drowsy when I'm with you
you make it hard
to sleep—you sleep
so soundly
it's the only sound I hear
you sleep so hard.

I just want to fall asleep on a pimpled green lawn where
children are routinely folded into lawn chairs and leisure
suits are set ablaze in moments of passion.

These are current events.

Screeching pistols
from shore
to shiny shore.
See what I mean?
See. Me?

I just blinked.
What?   Tune in tomorrow.

PINK SYNCOPATION

Stranded without a salt lick
I taped two crew-length sports socks
over my eyes with duct tape
and donned a pair of deer antlers.
The socks were salty so they swelled up.
Wandering around the mall
I looked just like a deer
with silver bread stuck to my eyes.
I have it all on videotape.

CINNAMON POEM

After yet another
cinnamon roll
am I really going to swim
in the ocean and
shake my hair
in the salt
water?
I don't think
it matters a whole helluva lot
what I do—
In fact
an oscillating fan
blows left
then right
and that's interesting enough
for me
while clouds come
and go
rain falls
and then dries—
The hair on my thick hands
is blonder,
a black swimsuit
with neon pink and green stripes—
The coral lampshade has too many lumps
for the surface of my skull—
Wait.
There's a sound:
it's wind through
the palms
and that's fantastic.

UNBRONZED FRET

When I go into a megalithic
gaseteria in the middle of Iowa
my heart shakes, quakes, I'm baked!
I'm full of desire for the man pumping gas with his belly below
his belt
and a handkerchief mopping sweat
from his dazed midwestern skies.

I wanna slap him on the back
and say, "Doesn't it drive you crazy that we're all gonna die?"

I want to hug him and feel the gelatinous love of Mississippi
mud...tuned down
to a low D...
I want to kiss his lips...
I DO and I AM and I'm holding him
right now!

I LOVE YOU!

Let me take you into the TCBY and buy
you a football helmet full of fat-free yogurt!

I love you man!
Let's eat candy corn together
and whisper something about

SOYBEAN GLOOM!

My Midwestern roots keep me from climbing a tree...say what?
I want to SHOUT
I AM shouting I turn my back
my front I go round and round the gas pump in the heart of

America looking for one love.

I want to put my arms around the heart beat of America and say,
"Things are really FUCKED UP!"

We're identical replicas of each other
living the same lives in the same towns
drawn from the same blueprints!

HEY!
There's something kinda scary going on... There's something
kinda scary going on...RIGHT HERE

Middle America is the smell
of meat on the grill and
my eyes have seen
the glory
of the coming
of the burger
bring me another beer!
Stand clear
while Dad lights
the grill
with an
electric match
POW!
and I'm suddenly surrounded by
the glorious smell
of forever and ever and ever...

I want to kiss your wacky stacks of gravy slacks in the Wal-
Mart...
How can you possibly be depressed when you're surrounded by
12 acres of brown slacks right on Interstate 80?

I want to kiss your lips, your corn, your beans... I want to taste
the sweat on your lip
as you stand at the gas pump on the Fourth of July eyeing the
        little girl

with ice cream melting down her hand

YOU ARE FREE
AND YOU CAN EAT ALL YOU WANT
BECAUSE THIS IS A FREE BUFFET
AND I BRING YOU GLAD TIDINGS FROM THE
SALAD BAR AT SHONEY'S
I BRING YOU GLAD TIDINGS FROM THE GAS PUMP
FROM THE MEAT STUMP
FROM THE HOLLOW-EYED YOGURT CLERK
LEERING AT ME!

HEY!
I don't have much time
I gotta go home and kiss
so many people
right on the lips
because everyone is SO close,
SO clueless
and SO far away
at the very
         same
                 time!

Go ahead and
whisper to ME America,
"I love you!"

RIPSNORT

TODD COLBY

BULL BY THE HORNS

TAKING THE BULL BY THE HORNS
AND LIFTING THE BULL UP BY THE HORNS
AND TAKING THE BULL BY THE HORNS
AND TAKING THE BULL UP BY THE HORNS AND
LIFTING THE BULL
BY THE HORNS UP INTO THE AIR
TAKING THE BULL UP BY THE HORNS AND LIFTING
IT INTO THE AIR
THE BULL IS HOISTED INTO THE AIR
BY THE HORNS
THE BULL IS CAUGHT BY THE HORNS
THE BULL IS TAKEN BY THE HORNS AND TOSSED
INTO THE AIR THE BULL IS CAUGHT
THE BULL IS CAUGHT BY THE HORNS AND TOSSED
KICKING INTO THE AIR
JUST LIFTING THE BULL BY THE HORNS AND TOSS-
ING IT INTO THE RIVER
TO JUST THROW THE BULL INTO THE RIVER
BY THE HORNS
TO JUST THROW THE BULL A LONG WAY
TO JUST TOSS THE BULL AWAY
TO TAKE THE BULL BY THE HORNS AND THROW IT
KICKING INTO THE RIVER
KICKING AND SCREAMING AND SNORTING
AND NOT BEING UPSET THAT THE BULL IS UPSET
THAT IT IS BEING
TAKEN BY THE HORNS AND IS DRIPPING GOO
FROM THE RING IN ITS NOSE
AND THE BULL IS SNORTING
AND MAKING WILD SOUNDS
AND TAKING THE BULL
BY THE HORNS ANYWAY AND TOSSING IT
INTO THE RIVER

TO JUST THROW THE BULL INTO THE RIVER
TO JUST THROW THE BULL A VERY LONG WAY
THE KICKING AND SCREAMING AND SNORTING
BULL IS IN THE RIVER
YOU WANTED THE BULL THE FUCK OUT OF YOUR
LIFE SO YOU TOOK IT
BY THE HORNS AND TOSSED IT INTO THE RIVER
YOU TOOK THE BULL BY THE HORNS
YOU CAUGHT THE BULL BY THE HORNS
YOU STOOD NEXT TO THE RIVER
YOU LIFTED THE BULL
BY THE HORNS OVER THE FENCE
NEXT TO THE RIVER
YOU TOSSED THE BULL INTO THE WATER
BY THE HORNS
YOU WANTED THE BULL THE FUCK OUT AND NOW
IT'S THE FUCK OUT
IT'S A LONG WAY TO TOSS A BULL BUT YOU DID IT
YOU TOOK IT BY THE HORNS
I HOPE YOU'RE HAPPY
I HOPE YOU ARE VERY HAPPY
I HOPE YOU'RE WONDERFULLY HAPPY
AND HAVING A GOOD TIME
WATCHING THE BULL IN THE WATER
YOU TOSSED THE BULL IN THE WATER
BY THE HORNS
YOU WATCHED THE HOOVES
THRASHING IN THE AIR AND WATER
AND ITS HORNS BOBBING AND I HOPE YOU HAVE
A VERY PLEASANT DAY
A WONDERFULLY PLEASANT DAY
A HAPPY AND A VERY PLEASANT
AND A VERY HAPPY DAY

COWBOY POEM

I am winning
they are losing
school is delayed
they're about to make a touchdown
they went to get milk

Outside it's
white and green and brown
it's a snow day, so to speak

They just made a first down
Hardee's is four miles from here
and now for something pretty:
flowers, honey, trees, snow, and rain

That's a mouthful

Pizza is my favorite food
red and black are my favorite colors
Friday is my favorite day
December is my favorite month
thanks for your attention.

Written with Alex Smith, 9 years old.

WHAT'S FOR DREAMER?

Leek compote

Roasted squab with cabbage,
mashed potatoes and white truffle oil.

Charlotte pears with raspberry puree.

Grilled salmon with bright
sorrel sauce and green lentils.

Seared venison with truffle oil
and parsnip-almond tartlet.

Fennel emulsion

Marinated shrimp with horseradish
chili oil and mixed greens.

Nicely browned skate with sweet
turnip puree.

Potato and onion cake.

Potato mouseline with peppy
horseradish-mustard sauce.

Sauteed bananas with a
star anise parfait.

BRONZE POEM

walking like a drunk
in two feet of snow
the city is a winter wonderland
I'm so clumsy with my heart
a real nerd
climbing the steps
and fighting the slip
on the flipside—the crush
of water apples
in the green vein
of stillness over
and over again
I wonder what to
do with all these bronze crayons...
melt them into
a shield?
serve them on
envelopes as seals?
a bronze bit
for a Budweiser clydesdale?

oh hell
I don't want any more crayons
and for that matter
I don't want any more bullies
or creeps telling me what to do
I don't have the time
I've lost the mantle
of good faith
I only have one soft wish:
to see them retreat
before I put them to sleep
with my bronze bat, yep.

COME

DISHES, SAXOPHONE,
A COLLISION.

THE TASTY MIX OF GRAPE BUBBLE YUM
AND CHALK.

THE SMELL OF FARTS.
BAD EGGERS. LINGERING
GAS POISON. METHANE
THUNDER PUMP.
FLATULENT 1994 THUMP,
FIZZ OUT MY HOLE.

MY SWAMP SMELL
HOTNESS. FIST IN HELL
CANAL OF DISGUSTING THUNDER,
WHITE NOISE OF HUMILIATING
COME.

BLOOD SPUR AND
HOT FUCK SAUCE.

THE EROTIC SPONGE.

I AM MECHANICAL AND SOLDIER-LIKE
IN MY SPLENDOR AND CONFUSION.

RECLINING HOT ORGASM THRASH UNDER A
THIN, MUSCULAR, MOON.

MOTORCYCLE DADDY
AND HOT PANTS MAMA
CHAIN SHARKS TO THE CLAVICLE
OF AN UNSUSPECTING FUCK TOY.

METAL SHAVINGS.

COME WHILE WATCHING THE BRADY BUNCH
SHEETS WITH HOT DIME COME SPOTS.

ANOTHER KISS POEM

I caught a frog.

I got a thick piece of cardboard,

a few stick pins,

and a razorblade used for stripping

paint off glass.

I pinned down the frog's four legs

and made an incision down its

soft white underside.

At that very moment

my mother ran out the side door screaming,

"IS THIS WHAT YOU'VE LEARNED

FROM THAT ROCK GROUP KISS?"

CAKE

I'm so full of cake
If I ate any more cake
I'd have to vomit first
I could eat a cake a day
Sometimes two three cakes
In a single day

I LOVE CAKE

I can't be any clearer than that

I LOVE CAKE

I could eat every cake in New York City
I can't even go into bakeries anymore
Because I'll eat all the cake

I'll say, "Where's the cake?
I love cake
Get me some cake!"

And they'll say,
"We know how much you love cake
And we know that you very rarely
Have the money to buy our cake
So you can't come in here because
You can't afford the cake
But you love cake
So get out of here
You can not have any cake
You don't have the money
To buy any of our cake!"

I'll punch some ass for cake
Gimme all your cake

I WANT CAKE

I WANT YOUR CAKE

GIMME ALL YOUR CAKE

I LOVE CAKE

.

THE BOSS

I DON'T WANT TO GET ANOTHER JOB
I WANT TO SLEEP AND READ
AND WRITE IN MY JOURNAL
AND PLAY MUSIC
AND DANCE
AND NEVER LIFT ANOTHER FINGER FOR ANOTH-
ER BOSS AND NEVER GET IN ANOTHER ARGU-
MENT WITH A BOSS AND NEVER SMACK THE BACK
OF THE BOSS'S HEAD
BUT THAT'S NOT UNUSUAL
BECAUSE I WATCH A LOT OF TV.

I'M YOUR JELLY FISH BOY-MAN
I'M KICKED AND CORNERED, BLOTCHED AND
SPENT

I SPREAD MY JELLY THIGHS WITH GASOLINE

I'M A GOOD BOY, I'M FULL OF SUNSHINE AND BEEF

I'M THE BINGO BOY, I'M NOT FULL OF SHIT

I ZOOM—
I BOOM—

I ZOOM AND BOOM RIGHT INTO THE FRYING PAN
WHERE THE AIR IS CHICKEN FLAVORED—
WHERE MY ROBE SMELLS LIKE CHICKEN SOUP

I'M LOST IN THE FOREST OF METAL OBJECTS...
HAVE YOU EVER HAD TO WORK IN A FOREST OF
METAL OBJECTS?

THEY GAVE ME PILLS WHEN I COULDN'T SLEEP...
THEY GAVE ME MEDALLIONS WHEN I DID A GOOD

JOB... BUT THEY WERE MEDALLIONS OF BEEF, GOD DAMMIT!

RIP THROUGH ME WITH THE PURPLE BLADES OF YOUR DEMON POISON I WANT THE DOCTOR TO CUT THESE DEMONS OUT OF MY MOUTH. I WANT THEM OUT!
GET OUT!
DEMONS!
GET OUT!
OUT, OUT, OUT!

GET AWAY FROM ME!
I'M IN A BAD MOOD!
I'M TRYING TO MAKE SENSE!

THE BATHROOM WAS SHAKING
THE SOAP WAS THROBBING
THERE WAS BLOOD ON THE FLOOR
THERE WAS BLOOD ON THE BOSS'S FACE

IF THE MASTER DEMON COMES TO YOUR TABLE TELL HIM THAT YOU ARE NOT AFRAID...TELL HIM THAT YOU ARE THE BOSS!

MY MOUTH TASTES LIKE RANCID MEAT...
IT'S THE BOSS, REMEMBER?

FIRE, GET OUT...GET OUT, FIRE! THERE'S A FIRE IN HERE, GET OUT!

I DON'T NEED ANOTHER ANGST-RIDDEN-POP-ANTHEM TO EXPLAIN MY FEELINGS I NEED TO PUNCH THE BOSS IN THE FACE

STOP THE CAMARO...GET OUT OF THE CAMARO...PAY ATTENTION...

I'VE BEEN CAUGHT WITH MY PANTS WRAPPED AROUND MY HEAD... MY HEAD IS ACTUALLY A FIST IN A CUP...

I'M HAPPY AS LARRY
I JACK OFF ON MY OLD FOOTBALL JERSEY

I WAS IN A STAR-SPANGLED RODEO GETTING
CARDS AND LETTERS
       FROM PEOPLE I DON'T EVEN KNOW...

I WAS OUT TO LUNCH!
I WAS AWARE OF A FILTHY ANIMAL IN MY MIDST...
IT WAS THE BOSS!

I WAS DOING MY LAUNDRY THE OTHER DAY
AND I WAS SURE THE BOSS SPIT ON MY CLOTHES
WHILE THEY WERE IN THE DRYER
SO I SPRAYED THE BOSS WITH PEPPER GAS

DON'T GIVE ME NONE OF YOUR GOD SASS
I GOT MUSTARD ALL OVER MY SLACKS
I WANT TO BOX THE EARS OF THE BOSS
I WANT TO BOX THE EARS OF THE
       NUMBER ONE GOD!

I'M A SUPERFREAK
I CAN'T TALK WITH A CHROME PLATED SHOE-
HORN IN MY MOUTH BECAUSE MY MOUTH IS
OVER THE BOSS'S MOUTH

I'M RUNNING THROUGH A FOREST OF METAL
OBJECTS, I'M LOST! WHATEVER I KNEW ABOUT
ANYTHING, I'VE LOST! IT'S GONE!

I THOUGHT I COULD TREMBLE IN CODED VIBRA-
TIONS I THOUGHT I COULD SEND MESSAGES TO
THE BOSS WITHOUT SPEAKING I THOUGHT I GES-
TURED WITH A SENSE OF PURPOSE I THOUGHT I
WAS REFINED!

I-AM-THE-WEBER-GRILL-GOD! AND
I-WHACK-DEEP-BLUE-THROAT-WOUNDS ON THE
BOSS'S NECK!

SLOW DOWN THE CAMARO,
I WANT TO GET OUT,
I PROMISE I WON'T DO NO MORE DRUGS!
JUST STOP THE CAMARO! STOP IT! STOP THE
CAMARO!

THE MASTER DEMON COULD BE THE BUSBOY
STANDING AT YOUR TABLE HE COULD BE YOUR
FARMER FRIEND
HE COULD BE THE PHILLIES' FIRST BASEMEN
HE COULD BE YOUR BOSS!

THE BEAST IS IN ME
AND I AM IN THE INDUSTRY

DON'T GIVE ME NONE OF YOUR GOD SASS, BOSS
DON'T THROW YOUR SUGAR BOOMERANG AT ME,
BOSS DON'T FILL YOUR BALLOONS WITH JELLY
AND TOSS THEM AT ME, BOSS

BRING BACK THE ROLLER DERBY!
I WANT TO BE IN THE ROLLER DERBY WITH THE
BOSS I WANT TO THROW MY ELBOW INTO HIS JAW
AS WE SKATE AROUND THE OVAL TRACK...I-WANT-
TO-PUT-THE-BOSS-DOWN-ON-THE-RINK!

THERE'S NOTHING WRONG WITH ME-

I'M NOT ANXIOUS
I JUST WANT TO CONTROL THE BOSS FOR ONE DAY
I-AM-THE-WEBBER-GRILL-GOD
IS THAT OKAY BOSS?

I WANT THE STAR SPANGLED BANNER ALL DAY! I
WANT TO SERVE YOU ALL THE TIME!
I FOUND A DREAM, AND
I-AM-THE-WEBBER-GRILL-GOD! AND
I-DANCE-MY-WEBBER-GRILL-DANCE...FOR THE
BOSS!

BLUE POEM

BLUE WINE STAINS ABOVE MY BLUE EYES.
THE BLUE SKY. MY BLUE CHILLY LIPS. MY
BLUE SHIRT. MY BLUE ROBE. MY THANKFULNESS
AT THEIR FORGETTING. MY MOTION WHICH
IS PURE AND BLUE. IT IS ORANGE TOO BUT MOST-
LY
BLUE. ORANGE JUICE AND BLUEBERRIES. THE
BLUE
FIELD. BLUE MIDNIGHT. BLUE CHRISTMAS.
ORANGE
HEADLIGHTS. ORANGE TOO. NOT JUST BLUE.
        BLUE MOON. ORANGE
YOU GLAD YOU USE DIAL? BLUE AND STILL.
        THE BLUE BICYCLE.
THE BLUE GUITAR. THE BLUE VEINS. ORANGINA.
BLUE. BLUE. STILL BLUE.

Biography

TODD COLBY is a poet, lyricist, vocalist and actor. This is his third published work, following *Ripsnort* (1994), *Cush* (1995), all published by Soft Skull. His poetry has appeared in numerous anthologies, most recently: *Heights of the Marvelous* (St. Martin's Press, 2000) which he also edited, and *Verses that Hurt* (St. Martin's, 1997).

Todd has performed his poetry on PBS, MTV and Canada's Much Music Network. He has produced many collaborative books and paintings with the artist David Lantow. Their collaboration, *Blown*, a limited edition of lithographs and poems, is at the Brooklyn Museum of Art and The Museum of Modern Art special collections libraries.

Todd has taught poetry workshops and co-coordinated the Wednesday Night Reading Series with Jo Ann Wasserman at The Poetry Project at St. Mark's Church in New York City. He was the lyricist and vocalist for the now-legendary New York band Drunken Boat. He is the cofounder with Jordan Trachtenberg of the Poemfone (212-631-4234). He is a founding member (with Marianne Vitale and Michael Portnoy) of the performance group The Yogurt Boys. Currently he is the poetry editor for *Food and Water Journal*.